COUNTRIES

Spain

Ruth Thomson

PowerKiDS
press.
New York

Published in 2011 by The Rosen Publishing Group Inc.
29 East 21st Street, New York, NY 10010

First Edition

Editor: Steve White-Thomson
Designer: Amy Sparks
Picture Researchers: Ruth Thomson/
  Steve White-Thomson
Series Consultant: Kate Ruttle
Design Concept: Paul Cherrill

Library of Congress Cataloging-in-Publication Data

Thomson, Ruth, 1949-
Spain / by Ruth Thomson. -- 1st ed.
      p. cm. -- (Countries)
Includes index.
ISBN 978-1-4488-3278-1 (library binding)
1. Spain--Juvenile literature. 2. Spain--Social life and
customs--Juvenile literature. I. Title.
DP17.T56 2011
946--dc22
                              2010023715

Photographs:
Alamy: Barbara Boensch 15; Corbis: David Lefranc/Kipa front
cover; Dreamstime: Noam Armonn 11l; Photolibrary: Christophe
Boisvieux 19; Shutterstock: Ana del Castillo 1/10, Elena Aliaga
2/8, Jo Chambers 5, Konstantin Shishkin 6, David Hughes 7,
dlnicolas 9, Mircea Bezergheanu 11r, Botond Horváth 12,
mangojuicy 13b, Tim Tran 13t, Marek Slusarczyk 14, Vinicius
Tupinamba 17, Audi Dela Cruz 16tr, Carolina 16mr, Somatuscan
16br, irabel8 16bl, Jonas San Luis 16tl, Matt Trommer 18,
Ashiga 20, Bill Florence 21, Dusan Po 22; Neil Thomson 23.

Manufactured in China
CPSIA Compliance Information: Batch #WAW1102PK: For Further Information
contact Rosen Publishing, New York, New York at 1-800-237-9932

Web Sites

Due to the changing nature of Internet
links, PowerKids Press has developed
an online list of Web sites related to
the subject of this book. This site is
updated regularly. Please use this link
to access this list:
http://www.powerkidslinks.com/cou/spain

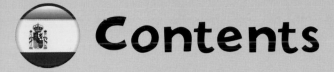# Contents

Where Is Spain?

Here is a map of Spain.

Spain is in southwest Europe.

Bay of Biscay

FRANCE

Bilbao

ANDORRA

P y r e n e e s

Duoro River

Ebre River

Lloret de Mar

Barcelona

PORTUGAL

Madrid

Minorca

Tajus River

Majorca

SPAIN

Valencia

Ibiza

Benidorm

Mediterranean Sea

Seville

Sierra Nevada

Malaga

Cadiz

Marbella

Torremolinos

Atlantic Ocean

EUROPE

ALGERIA

MOROCCO

Madrid is the capital of Spain.
It is in the center of the country.
The King of Spain has a palace there.

The Royal Palace has 2,800 rooms,
more than any other palace in Europe.

Land and Sea

The high Pyrenees mountains in the north are between Spain and France. There are dry plains in the center of the country and good farmland near the coasts.

In the winter, people go skiing and snowboarding in the Pyrenees.

Spain has long coasts. The north coast faces the Atlantic Ocean. The east and south coasts face the Mediterranean Sea.

The north is cool and rainy, so the land is very green.

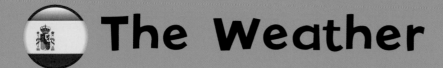

The Weather

Spain is the sunniest country in Europe. In the summer, the Mediterranean coast has 12 hours of sunshine every day.

Millions of tourists crowd the beaches. Many stay in big hotels.

In the winter, it is very cold on the
plains and near the mountains.
There is often heavy snow.

The tops of the Sierra Nevada mountains are
covered with snow for six months of the year.

Town and Country

Most Spanish people live in towns or cities. The shopping streets in the city centers are often closed to traffic.

Stores stay open late. In the early evening, people often take a stroll through the streets.

In the country, many Spanish farmers grow oranges, lemons, olives, sunflowers, or grapes. These crops ripen in the long, sunny days of summer.

Olive trees can live up to 500 years.

Orange blossoms smell very sweet.

Olive and orange trees are evergreens. They do not drop their leaves in the fall.

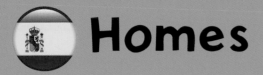

Homes

In towns and cities, many people
live in apartments or houses.
These rarely have yards,
but often have balconies instead.

The windows have shutters to keep out the hot sun.

In the north, apartments have glassed-in balconies. In the south, houses are white with thick walls and small windows.

The strong glass in these apartments in the north keep out wind and rain.

Houses in the south stay cool in the hot sun.

Shopping

People shop for food in supermarkets, indoor markets, and small shops.

Busy markets sell meat, fish, fruit, vegetables, and cheese.

The Spanish use euros and cents as their money.

14

There are modern shopping malls in big cities. These are open every day of the week until late at night.

This mall in Barcelona is by the sea. It has an aquarium and lots of stores.

Food

Cooking varies from one area of Spain to another. These are some popular dishes.

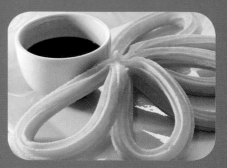

churros (doughnuts) and hot chocolate

empanada (meat or fish pie with onions and bell peppers)

fabada (beans and pork soup) from the north

gazpacho (cold tomato soup) from the south

paella (rice with seafood and chicken) from Valencia

After work, many people eat hot and cold snacks called tapas with a drink. The Spanish eat dinner very late.

On warm summer nights, people eat and drink at tables outside.

Musicians often play their instruments at open-air cafés.

Sports

Spanish people love their sports. Basketball, tennis, cycling, and soccer are popular.

Real Madrid has won the European Cup nine times, more than any other soccer team.

Spain won the 2010 World Cup. They like to play exciting soccer!

In northeast Spain, people play a
ball game called pelota. Two teams
take turns hitting a rubber ball
against a high wall.

Players wear a glove with a basket on the end.
They catch and throw the ball with it.

Festivals

Every town and village in Spain
holds its own festival, called a fiesta.
The most important celebrations
are in Holy Week before Easter.

Men parade through the streets
with holy sculptures on floats.

At festivals in the south, some people dance the flamenco. The dancers click castanets and stamp their feet in time to guitar music.

Female flumenco dancers always wear long, frilly dresses and high-heeled shoes.

Speak Spanish!

¡Hola! *(o-la)*	Hello
¿Que tal? *(kay tal)*	How are you?
Vale *(bah-lay)*	OK
¡Adiós! *(ad-yoss)*	Goodbye
Por favor *(por fav-or)*	Please
Gracias *(grath-yass)*	Thank you
Si *(see)*	Yes
No *(no)*	No
Me llamo... *(may ya-mo)*	My name is...

Spain's flag has the Spanish coat of arms on it.

A Spanish Ball Game

Spanish children call this ball game "Burro." This means "donkey" in Spanish.

1. One player bounces a ball and hits it against a wall with one hand.

2. The second player must catch the ball before it bounces.

3. The second player then bounces the ball and hits it against the wall for the first player to catch.

4. If you don't catch the ball before it bounces, you get the letter "B" (of Burro). Every time you miss the ball, you get another letter of "Burro."

The first player to complete the word "Burro" loses the game.

Glossary and Further Information

apartment a home with rooms all on the same level of a building

balcony a platform on the outside of a building with railings or a wall around it

capital the city in a country where the government is

castanets two shells made of hard wood that dancers click together in their hands

market a place with stalls where people buy and sell things

plains large, flat areas of land

tourist someone who travels for fun or on vacation

Books

Let's Visit Spain
by Susie Brooks
(PowerKids Press, 2009)

Living in: Spain
by Su Kent
(Sea to Sea Publications, 2007)

Spain: A Question and Answer Book
by Kremena Spengler
(Capstone Press, 2005)

Index